All Scripture references taken from the KJV of the Holy Bible, unless otherwise indicated.

THE INTANGIBLES: ***God-Given Gifts That Empower Your Life*** by Dr. Marlene Miles

Freshwater Press 2026

Freshwaterpress9@gmail.com

ISBN: 978-1-971933-26-9

Paperback Version

Table of Contents

THE INTANGIBLES

God-Given Gifts That Empower Your Life

Man's greatest powers are not dramatic, this is why they may be so easily dismissed.

GREAT & PRECIOUS

Whereby are given unto us exceeding great and precious promises: that by these ye might be partakers of the divine nature, having escaped the corruption that is in the world through lust.
(2 Peter 1:4)

God has given us many gifts and were I to start to name them, I couldn't name them all. However, I will list many because, for the purposes of this book, I want us to become aware of how blessed we really are.

God created man in His own image and likeness and gave man Dominion. In order to be in Dominion man needs Authority. God has crowned man with Glory & Honor. Here, crowned must mean that along with Dominion we have a throne--, not one throne, but each of God's children has his own throne as we are little k, kings and He is the King of Kings. Man is on Earth with a purpose, working toward his own destiny, as well as the collective destinies that he is attached to, the collective destiny of man in the church as the Bride of Christ.

We are appointed other gifts, talents, skills, abilities, and even a star. We are given other gifts such as those that represent the Fruit of the Spirit such as Love, Joy, A deep-seated sense of happiness rooted in faith (Galatians 5:22). And, Peace which is a tranquil state of mind and spirit, regardless of circumstances, that surpasses understanding (Philippians 4:7).

We each are appointed a star and in our star is our health, marriage, abundance, wealth, education, children. God has given us everything that pertains to life and Godliness. And if that had not been enough, we read in the Word that even with all He had given David, if that had been too little, if that had not been enough, then David should have told the Lord God, and God then would have given him more. Even to the desires of his own heart.

We are given virtues such as Wisdom - The ability to discern and apply knowledge effectively Insight and understanding that guide decisions and actions (James 1:5). God says He will give that liberally to anyone who asks. Understanding - Insight into the deeper meanings of faith and life. Counsel - The gift of providing guidance and support to others. Fortitude - Strength and courage to face challenges and adversity. Knowledge - A deep understanding of spiritual truths and doctrines. Piety - A heartfelt devotion and reverence towards God. ear of the Lord - A profound respect and awe for God's majesty.

Love - The greatest gift, embodying selfless care and compassion for others. (1 Corinthians 13:13). And other Fruit of the Spirit, including Kindness - A disposition to be generous and considerate towards others (Ephesians 4:32). Faithfulness - A steadfast loyalty and trust in God and His promises (Galatians 5:22). Goodness - A moral quality that reflects God's character in our actions (Galatians 5:22). Gentleness - A humble and meek spirit that responds with compassion (Galatians 5:23). Self-Control - The ability to govern one's desires and impulses (Galatians 5:23).

Power? Power belongs to God but He has given us all power to accomplish useful, necessary, Godly things.

The Fall of Man was the day the devil made the first trade and man has been trading ever since. What are we trading? That is what this book is about. What does the vendor have? Why do we want it? And what is the cost; what does he want from us?

REAL IN THE SPIRIT

Everything listed in the debut chapter is invisible. Yes, it has visible, tangible results and outcomes, but these things are not things that you can touch, feel, taste, see, smell in and of themselves. They are intangible to man--, well to most men. So, the man who ignores, refuses to see, or haphazardly stewards over these *intangibles*, even though they belong to him, or belong to his Peace, may end up making trades that he doesn't know he is making. In so doing, he may also not know how bad of a deal he made.

The Intangibles are realities that are not visible, not weighable, not measurable by our natural senses or by modern metrics. Yet, these intangibles govern outcomes, shape Peace, and determine authority.

We can look at them as pre-material.

Scripture treats them as *real first*, not symbolic.

> The things which are seen were not made of things which do appear. (Hebrews 11)

They don't produce immediate relief although they are quite powerful and useful, else God wouldn't have given them to us. To become aware of them requires discernment instead of reaction. For these reasons, man may ignore them, discount them, disregard them. Often, he will simply yield or lose them because he doesn't even know they exist. He may stupidly trade them, trample them, or mismanage them. Would you throw an expensive pair of shoes or sneakers into the corner of your house somewhere? No, you'd keep them together, organized and even protected in their own box or space. And that's because you can see them and they bring you immediate gratification when you use them.

But the intangibles that God gives us, far more precious than the things that re seen, are we not using those things and using them well, and still wondering why life feels heavy, noisy, or unstable?

Trade? Yes, people trade with these items all the time. How? Someone offended you, so now you want to hate them or plan revenge. You've traded love and forgiveness, both worth far more than what you want. You've traded for hate.

What man calls intangible the spirit sees as real. There are things in your life that cannot be measured, yet they determine everything. You cannot weigh them, photograph them, or prove them in a spreadsheet. Yet, when they shift, your entire world shifts with them.

You have felt this before. A room was the same. The people were the same. The circumstances had not changed. But something invisible had changed — and you knew it. Maybe it was that Peace was gone. Or, clarity was disturbed. Alignment felt off. Words landed differently. Decisions felt heavier.

Nothing tangible had collapsed. But something governing had moved. Most people do not have language for this. They say, "I just feel weird about it." "Something's off." "I don't know why, but this doesn't sit right."

Then they override it. They proceed. They push. They rationalize. Later on, sometimes much later, they discover that what they ignored was not a feeling. It was structure; it was a structural shift.

Scripture does not treat these realities as abstract. From the beginning, the invisible precedes the visible.

The things which are seen were not made of things which do appear.
(Hebrews 11)

Before land existed, order existed. Before fruit appeared, alignment was established. Before blessing manifested, covenant was spoken. Modern culture reveres what can be measured. Scripture reveres what governs.

This is the divide.

What man calls intangible, Scripture calls real. No matter what man calls it, that does not make it so. It is real in the spirit realm and the beings in the spirit, especially the enemy of our souls is using it, like a man who acquires land, acre by acre until he's bought up all in a town or city, or state or country if he could. It's real.

People who do not think things are real will disregard those things or ignore them, often to their own shortfall or demise.

Peace is not an object that can be held in our hand. However, I remember my mother saying, "Hold your peace." Which really meant, be quiet, don't say anything, especially not what you were planning to say. Peace does not announce itself loudly, yet when it is gone, the problems begin to mount. Productivity suffers. Relationships strain. Authority weakens. Sleep is disturbed. Decisions become impulsive.

Peace is invisible — but its absence is loud. The enemy of our souls is out to steal a man's peace. How can he steal something that is invisible? It's visible to him, that's how.

Consider discernment. You cannot show it to someone. You cannot quantify it. But you have experienced the moment when you knew something was wrong before evidence appeared. That was not imagination; that was perceptual authority. These particular intangibles are governing conditions; they are conditions under which self-governance is possible.

They are invisible, they are easily dismissed, especially if a man lets himself get distracted. We know distraction is the #1 devil tactic.

The tragedy of any tragic modern life is not lack of power; it is the consistent mismanagement of what cannot be seen. Man chases outcomes while neglecting conditions. He pursues tangible increase while ignoring intangible order. He seeks authority while disregarding alignment.

Then he wonders why things leak.

This book will name what has always been present. It will restore seriousness to what has been casually treated. It will teach you to steward what you already possess. The most powerful forces in your life are not dramatic. They are quiet. Sometimes God hides things for our protection, and for the protection of the thing hidden. But who is roaming about searching to steal, kill, and destroy? The enemy of our souls, and if he can't pounce directly, he will start with a trade—well a man may think it's a trade, it's a theft because any of your intangibles is priceless and the devil never offers the real or fair price for anything. He can't. He didn't make it and it is priceless – so it should never be sold or traded in the first place.

So, these discreet things are necessary for your life and your godliness. They are things that pertain to your Peace and your success in life. They are structural. They are entrusted to you--, to man.

Whether you acknowledge them or not, they are governing you in the sense that you need them for proper governance.

CORE INTANGIBLES

Those in the spirit, even our spiritual enemies treat what we may see as intangible as REAL They are tangible to them.

1. **Peace** is not a mood. It is **a** governing condition. It is intangible to us, but spiritually it is a real thing.

"My peace I give unto you…"
(John 14)

We see that Peace can be given, kept, forfeited, lost, given away. We then know it should be guarded. However, people trade Peace every day for access, approval, urgency, money, and or avoidance.

2. **Discernment** is not intuition; it is perceptual authority. Scripture treats lack of discernment as *danger*, not ignorance. When discernment is ignored, lust and appetite governs, emotion is running the show, pressure governs, be it peer-pressure or fear-pressure.

God says He will never leave or forsake us, so if God is not nearby, with you, in you, that means you sat Him down somewhere like He was a toy idol.

Discernment must be turned on, used, sharpened. However, a trade is when a person may decide that they want to go here or there, have some fun, let loose, do what everyone else is doing ,so they turn off the Holy Spirit, grieve or quench the Holy Spirit, stop listening to the Holy Spirit. This is a trade: fun for discernment. Do you see how lop-sided this is already. Who in their right mind would be willing to lose the Holy Spirit, especially if it was difficult for you to receive in the first place, set Him down somewhere and go back to the party life you were living before you got saved? Especially if you don’t know if you can just pick Him up again. Can you?

3. Timing is an intangible that controls fruitfulness. You could take the same action with bad or wrong timing and have a completely different outcome than needed or anticipated.

Man says, "Why didn't this work?" Scripture says, "it wasn't time." Sometimes what is said is, *It's too late; that season is over.* Ignoring timing is disregard for order.

4. Under Authority are Boundaries. Boundaries are invisible — but enforceable. They are not walls. They are jurisdiction lines. When boundaries are treated casually, Peace leaks, authority erodes, resentment grows. Boundaries are an intangible that **protects tangibles**.

5. Under Power are Words. (more on power later). Words are intangible — yet Scripture treats them as containers, seeds, weapons, covenants, and contracts. Words outlive emotions. They establish environments. This is why Scripture never treats speech casually.

6. Alignment is not just agreement; it is directional unity. A person can be sincere and misaligned. That does not protect them. Misalignment silently drains strength, joy, and authority.

The most powerful things entrusted to man cannot be seen — which is why they are so easily mismanaged.

Authority teaches what man is entrusted with. **The Intangibles** teaches what governs that entrustment. Authority answers, *What has been placed under my charge?* This book about intangibles answers, *What conditions preserve or destroy my peace, clarity, and rule?*

Man ignores what he cannot see, then suffers under what he refused to steward. This explains stress, chaos, disorder, burnout, confusion, spiritual fatigue.

We live in a culture that pretty much measures everything, values only what can be proven. Society often mocks restraint as boring and dismisses peace as weakness. Yet people are exhausted. It’s not always that they lack power, but because they have mishandled what keeps power usable.

The Intangibles: this book is about man's superpowers (that he too often overlooks or ignores).

THE INTANGIBLES: MAN'S SUPERPOWERS

Jerry Seinfeld said that to a little boy, being a superhero is not a fantasy, it's a career option. Man is imbued with powers and superpowers. He must pay attention to them, learn to use them and be both authorized and anointed to use them.

When it comes to the *intangible* things of God, calling them *superpowers* is not childish. It is accurate language for dormant capacity. A "superpower" is real, you're born with it, it is custom made just for you and your purpose and destiny. It is powerful, but if we don't pay attention these abilities can be underutilized.

That describes many intangibles such as Peace, discernment, forgiveness, restraint, timing, authority, and self-governance as well as the list from the first chapter, and more that we will discuss later in this book. They are actual forces that are real in the spiritual realm that govern the outcomes of your life.

Scripture already teaches that power is not always visible at rest. Ability does not announce itself. Capacity often looks ordinary until pressure demands expression. The tragedy is not lack of power; the tragedy is unused design.

The Intangibles addresses the error where man ignores what cannot be measured. He may undervalue what cannot be seen, especially if he doesn't even believe it exists. It is error to trade what is precious and cannot be replaced. Wrongly, a man may mishandle what governs his own Peace--, all while assuming the "real" problems are external.

Our spiritual enemy knows these things are real and tangible (in the spirit) and so like in life, but if we don't see it, we think they are junk or things discardable. The enemy is trading all day long and one trade isn't all he's after. When he can't do a fell swoop, he will trade by increments, first this, then that, then the next thing, until then you're his or under his control. Think of a game of Monopoly, don't you buy one property at a time?

> The merchandise of gold, and silver, and precious stones, and of pearls, and fine linen, and purple, and silk, and scarlet, and all thyine wood, and all manner vessels of ivory, and all manner vessels of most precious wood, and of brass, and iron, and marble,
>
> And cinnamon, and odours, and ointments, and frankincense, and wine, and oil, and fine flour, and wheat, and beasts, and sheep, and horses, and chariots, and slaves, and souls of men.
>
> And the fruits that thy soul lusted after are departed from thee, and all things which were dainty and goodly are departed from thee, and thou shalt find them no more at all. (Revelations 18:12-14)

When a man trades something for appetite, he may not be simply trading away something he really wants. Most of the time man thinks he's not trading anything at all. He thinks he is just getting something – for nothing. To that man "nothing" may be an intangible, and one he desperately needs because he needs everything God has given him. But since these things re invisible in the natural and he thinks he's getting over or tricking—someone he doesn't think he's losing anything. He only thinks he is gaining.

But he may be trading trust, moral gravity, spiritual sensitivity, the ease of his household, the atmosphere of his home, or even his children's sense of stability. These things are intangible assets in the natural, but tangible in the spirit where the trade is being made. Once damaged, or lost, they take time to rebuild. This is why appetite feels small in the moment but massive in consequence.

Esau did not just trade stew for a birthright. He traded inheritance, structure, covenant standing, and generational positioning, because he undervalued what he held.

That's *Intangibles.*

Authority says: "You are entrusted." Intangibles says: "Some of what you hold cannot be seen — but it is weight-bearing." In a building, load-bearing studs and walls are not always shown as decorative beams. They are in the building of the edifice, but you don't see them. You can't touch them, so in that sense, they are intangible, but they are as important or more so than the rest of the house.

Authority is about structure. Intangibles is about invisible weight. “When a man trades something of higher order for appetite, he rarely loses a visible asset first. He loses invisible weight — and that loss echoes.

The most devastating trades in life are not material. They are intangible. In **AUTHORITY**, we talk about restoration through alignment. In ***Intangibles***, we talk about rebuilding invisible support structures. Authority defines the structure.

Intangibles explains what fills it.

Authority asks: *What has been entrusted to man?*

The Intangibles asks: *What enables man to keep what he has been entrusted with?* Authority without intangibles becomes harsh, brittle, exhausting and short-lived. Intangibles without authority become sentimental, passive, and underutilized. Together, they produce adult humanity.

When something is intangible—unseen, unfelt, or not easily measured—it is often overlooked by those to whom it is entrusted. Even spiritual gifts, virtues, or blessings can escape a person’s awareness if they do not present themselves in obvious or material ways. Without clear markers or tangible evidence, the value of these things can be underestimated or dismissed as insignificant, despite their profound impact on life's structure and meaning.

This tendency to miss the intangible can lead to their misuse or neglect. When a person fails to recognize the invisible support beams in their own life—such as faith, peace, or integrity—they may inadvertently weaken their own foundation. Spiritual resources, if not consciously valued and stewarded, can be traded away for fleeting comforts or immediate gratification, much like Esau's exchange of birthright for a bowl of stew. The loss is not always felt immediately, but the consequences echo across time, impacting not only the individual but also generations that follow.

Therefore, it is crucial to cultivate an awareness of the intangibles, to perceive their worth even when they cannot be seen or touched. True stewardship involves recognizing the unseen treasures we hold and actively preserving them, so that their benefits are not lost but multiplied throughout our lives and the lives of those connected to us.

This could be especially perilous to those who want to reinvent God, reinvent church or reinvent spirituality. The King James Version of the Bible may be looked at as, ‘that old thing,’ when really it is bearing a lot of weight. Younger people may put something away or just leave it on the dresser thinking it has little to no value, especially if they don’t even know what it does. A pocket watch? Grandpa’s pocket watch? What do I need that for? I have my cell phone. We should never remove the old landmarks because when a people don’t know how they got here or where they came from they may discount or disregard very important things. When we are supposed to be building line upon line, precept upon precept, not ‘throwing out the old,’ and bringing in the new.

Jesus didn’t come to do away with the Law, which was the Old Testament. He came to fulfill it. Jesus did not throw out the old landmark.

The younger generation does not always reject God. They reinvent Him. They rebrand Him. They simplify Him. They aestheticize Him. They “make Him relatable.” In doing so, they may too often discard reverence, structure, weight, patience, nuance, authority, and submission. Those are intangibles. They are not flashy.

They are not viral. They are not loud; but they are stabilizers.

Remove not the ancient landmark (Proverbs 22:28)

Preserving foundation is not about clinging to old hymns or discarding invisible boundaries you do not yet understand. Young innovators often remove boundaries before they comprehend why they were placed.

Ask for the old paths… and ye shall find rest. (Jeremiah 6:16)

The "old path" is not outdated. It is proven. The generation that refuses the old path does not lose excitement. They lose rest. That's the intangible. Peace. Stability. Soul-rest.

They chase expression. They lose equilibrium. The generation that rushes to reinvent God often removes boundaries it has not yet learned to respect. Ancient landmarks are not relics. They are stabilizers. The old paths are not restrictive. They are restful. You may gain relevance by removing them — but you will lose Peace.

BLESSINGS, O GOD

Blessing is not luck.
It is order rewarded.

Blessing becomes the *fruit* of covenants, authority, alignment and governance systems functioning correctly.

In the Bible, blessing means more than "nice things happening." The Hebrew word *barak* and the Greek word *makarios* both carry the sense of divine favor, empowerment, flourishing, and covenant alignment. Here is a structured list of biblical blessings, grouped by theme, with key Scriptures behind them.

1. The Blessing of God's Presence. The first and greatest blessing is God Himself. God walking with Adam (Genesis 3:8) "I will be with you" (Exodus 3:12) The Priestly Blessing (Numbers 6:24–26) "Blessed are the pure in heart, for they shall see God" (Matthew 5:8).

Core blessing: Access to God's presence.

2. Covenant Blessings. In the Book of Deuteronomy 28:1–14, blessings are tied to obedience: Blessed in the city and field. Blessed offspring. Blessed harvest. Victory over enemies. Established as a holy people. Prosperity and abundance. These are national and generational covenant blessings.

So, God will bless you and your generations, meaning His blessings transcend time.

3. The Beatitudes (Kingdom Blessings). In the Gospel of Matthew 5:3–12: Blessed are the poor in spirit. Blessed are those who mourn. Blessed are the meek. Blessed are those who hunger for righteousness. Blessed are the merciful. Blessed are the pure in heart. Blessed are the peacemakers. Blessed are the persecuted. These are character-based blessings, not circumstantial ones.

4. Spiritual Blessings in Christ found in the Epistle to the Ephesians 1:3 says, "Blessed be the God… who has blessed us with every spiritual blessing in heavenly places in Christ." These include: Election, Adoption, Redemption, Forgiveness, Sealing with the Holy Spirit, and Inheritance. These are positional blessings — tied to identity.

5. The Blessing of Wisdom, located in the Book of Proverbs 3:13: "Blessed is the one who finds wisdom." Blessings include: Long life, Peace, Stability, Favor. Wisdom itself is called a blessing.

6. The Blessing of Fruitfulness begins in Genesis and threads throughout the Bible. "Be fruitful and multiply" (Genesis 1:28). In blessing, I will bless thee (Genesis 22:17-19) Fruit of the womb (Psalm 127:3–5) Spiritual fruit (Galatians 5:22–23) Fruitfulness is a blessing, both physical and spiritual.

7. The Blessing of Peace. Peace, *shalom*, is not just calm; it is wholeness. "The Lord give you peace" (Numbers 6:26) "Blessed are the peacemakers" (Matthew 5:9) "Peace I leave with you" (John 14:27) Peace is covenant stability.

8. The Blessing of Righteousness from the Book of Psalms 1: "Blessed is the man who does not walk in the counsel of the wicked…" Blessings described there: Stability, like a tree planted by the rivers of water. Fruit in season. Prosperity in what he does. Righteous alignment brings rootedness.

9. The Blessing of Provision. Daily bread is a blessing, (Matthew 6:11). God supplying needs (Philippians 4:19). Abraham's livestock and wealth are definite blessings, (Genesis 13:2). Provision is blessing — but never meant to replace God.

10. The Blessing of Protection. "The Lord bless you and keep you" (Numbers 6:24). Psalm 91 promises deliverance from danger. "No weapon formed against you…" (Isaiah 54:17) Protection is a covenant benefit.

11. The Blessing of Children. Psalm 127: "Children are a heritage from the Lord." Abraham's promised seed, (Genesis 12). Children are called a reward and heritage.

12. The Blessing of Salvation. The ultimate New Testament blessing: Forgiveness of sins. Eternal life (John 3:16). Justification (Romans 5:1). Salvation is the culmination of blessing.

13. The Blessing of Suffering for Christ. Counterintuitive but Biblical: "Blessed are you when men revile you…" (Matthew 5:11). "If you suffer for righteousness, you are blessed." (1 Peter 3:14). Alignment with Christ, even in hardship, is called blessing.

14. The Blessing of Giving. Acts of the Apostles 20:35: "It is more blessed to give than to receive." Generosity activates blessing.

15. The Blessing of Obedience. James 1:25: "The one who does the word… will be blessed in what he does." Blessing follows alignment. In Scripture, blessing is usually: relational, that is, God with you. Covenantal, this is tied to alignment. Generational blessings flow forward. Blessings are governed, not random. Blessings can be either tangible, intangible, or both.

It is not just increase; it is ordered increase under divine authority. Blessing is what happens when authority, alignment, and presence are in right order.

These blessings can be intangible and then move into the natural as tangible. But they do not function the same way. Biblically, blessings move in layers:

- Spiritual (positional)
- Internal (transformational)
- Relational (covenantal)
- Material (circumstantial).

1. Intangible Blessings are Spiritual and Internal; they are real but not physically measurable.

A. Spiritual Position (Ephesians 1:3) "every spiritual blessing in heavenly places" These include: Adoption, Redemption, Forgiveness, Sealing by the Spirit, and Inheritance. You cannot weigh these. But they change everything.

B. Character-Based Blessings. Seen in the Beatitudes, (Matthew 5): Meekness, Mercy, Purity of heart, and Hunger for righteousness. These are internal conditions that carry external consequences.

C. Peace, Wisdom, Joy Peace (John 14:27) Wisdom (Proverbs 3:13). Joy (Romans 15:13). You cannot see Peace — but you can see its fruit. These are intangible in form, tangible in effect.

2. Tangible Blessings (Material / Natural); these show up physically.

A. Covenant Provision. In the Book of Deuteronomy 28, we see blessings of crops, livestock, and land. We are promised victory in battle, and fruit of the womb. These are clearly natural outcomes.

B. Children as heritage (Psalm 127). That is tangible.

C. Protection. Deliverance from danger. Our health is preserved. Enemies are restrained. Many times, these blessings are often visible only in hindsight.

In Scripture, the intangible usually governs the tangible. Order produces increase. Alignment produces stability. Wisdom produces prosperity. Peace produces longevity. The blessing is first structural, then material. That is why someone can have tangible wealth but not be biblically "blessed." It is why someone can suffer materially yet still be called, blessed.

Under the New Covenant, the emphasis shifts. The Old Testament highlights obedience. The NT centers: Reconciliation, Transformation, Eternal life, and Christlikeness. Material blessing is not removed — but it is not primary.

Biblically, some blessings are intangible in nature. Some blessings are tangible in manifestation. Most blessings are intangible at the root and tangible in their fruit. Blessing is invisible order that eventually becomes visible stability.

- **Authority** is what has been entrusted
- **The Intangibles** is when what governs what's entrusted
- **Blessing** is when what flows when governance is aligned

The Biblical pattern is:

1. Alignment (intangible)
2. Order (intangible)
3. Favor (intangible)
4. Fruit (tangible) If you invert that order, chaos enters.

Most biblical blessings are *intangible* at the root and tangible in their fruit.

The point is, partying tonight may erase the blessings of the next day. Yes, the enemy sows weeds at night, but he will send emissaries to defile or tempt a person into sin. Defiled means you are outside the gate to the city at least one whole day. That means the blessings for that day are not made available to you. Not only that, if there was a special blessing, a promotion, award, bonus or any such thing that you were due to receive on Tuesday, Monday night temptation put you into sin and without realizing it, you traded. Sin and fun for your blessing, bonus, increase, promotion.

In the case of physical blessing, the *intangible* that would support or sustain or usher it into the natural was traded away by sin, so your reward never arrived in the natural. Will the opportunity come around again? Only God knows. Repent. Pray. Ask.

THE ARCHITECTURE OF BLESSING

This chapter answers two major errors:

1. People who reduce blessing to money.
2. People who reduce blessing to a vague spiritual *feeling*.

Blessing is one of the most overused and least examined words in the language of faith. It is spoken casually, wished freely, claimed quickly, and measured almost entirely by visible outcome. If something increases, it is called a blessing. If something feels pleasant, it is called a blessing. If something relieves discomfort, it is labeled as a blessing. But Scripture treats blessing with far more precision.

In the Biblical world, blessing is not primarily about acquisition. It is about alignment. It is not random increase. It is ordered increase. It is not luck, nor mood, nor sentiment. It is empowerment flowing through covenant structure.

From the beginning, blessing follows order. In Genesis, fruitfulness does not precede alignment; it follows it. Creation itself unfolds in sequence. Separation. Structure. Naming. Placement. Then fruitfulness. The visible is built on the invisible. The tangible rests on the intangible.

When God blesses Abraham, the blessing is not merely livestock and land. It is covenant positioning. "I will be your God." "I will make of you a great nation." The tangible outcomes: descendants, wealth, and territory are manifestations of a relational alignment already established. The blessing is not the cattle. The blessing is the covenant that produces the cattle.

This pattern repeats throughout Scripture. In Deuteronomy, material prosperity is tied explicitly to obedience — not because God is transactional, but because blessing rests where order is maintained. When alignment breaks, tangible stability erodes. Not instantly. Not theatrically. But steadily.

The Psalms describe the blessed man not as the one with the most possessions, but as the one properly positioned. He does not walk in certain counsel. He does not stand in certain paths. He does not sit in certain seats. Instead, he delights in the law of the Lord. His stability is compared to a tree planted by rivers of water. The fruit appears in season, but the blessing is the placement. The roots are the unseen structure that allows fruit to come at the proper time.

By the time the New Testament opens, blessing shifts further inward. "Blessed are the poor in spirit." "Blessed are the meek." "Blessed are the merciful." These declarations in the Sermon on the Mount disrupt every superficial definition of blessing. None of these are immediately measurable. None are dramatic. Yet they are called, ***blessed***.

Why?

Because they describe internal alignment. They describe hearts positioned correctly under God's order. The fruit of that positioning may not be immediate comfort. It may not be visible success. But it is structural stability.

The Apostle Paul later writes that believers have been blessed "with every spiritual blessing in heavenly places." These blessings cannot be seen at all. Adoption. Redemption. Sealing. Inheritance. These are positional realities, not circumstantial ones. They precede material conditions. They define identity before they influence environment.

This reveals the architecture of blessing clearly: blessing begins intangible and becomes tangible when order is preserved.

Peace, Wisdom, discernment, alignment — these are intangible forms of blessing. They are not decorative. They are governing. Where they remain intact, tangible stability tends to follow. Where they are ignored or traded, tangible instability eventually appears.

This is why a person can possess wealth and not be blessed. Tangible increase without intangible order is not blessing; it is accumulation. And it is why another person may suffer materially yet still be called, ***blessed*** — because alignment remains intact.

Blessing is not something chased. It is something maintained.

It rests where covenant alignment rests. It abides where peace is guarded. It strengthens where discernment is honored. It multiplies where order is not violated.

When the intangible structure is preserved, the tangible expression becomes sustainable.

When people try to fix visible fruit without examining invisible roots that will not work. They seek increased outcomes without restoring internal order. They pray for blessing while neglecting alignment. Then they wonder why increase does not hold.

Blessing is not fragile. But it is structured.

The invisible governs the visible. Always.

To understand the intangibles is to understand the foundation upon which blessing rests. To protect the intangibles is to protect the conditions in which blessing can remain.

THE LAYERS OF BLESSING

Layer 1: Positional (Spiritual) Adoption, redemption, inheritance. (Ephesians 1). These are invisible but permanent.

Layer 2: Internal. Peace, Wisdom, joy (Proverbs, John 14, Romans 15). These are intangible but experiential.

Layer 3: Relational. Covenant stability Presence of God. Alignment under authority. These are invisible but structural.

Layer 4: Tangible. Provision. Protection Fruitfulness. Increase. These are visible — but not primary.

The Critical thing is that the intangible governs the tangible. When Peace is disturbed, discernment is ignored, alignment is broken, tangible blessing begins to erode. Not because God is moody. It is because order has shifted.

The centurion understood intangible alignment because he was properly under authority, his words carried tangible effect. Blessing followed structure. That's order.

Blessing is about governance. Blessing is not something you chase. It is something that rests where order remains. When intangible alignment is preserved, tangible blessing is sustained. Blessing follows structure.

For those who ask why you are not blessed as you think you should be. After all, you quote the promises. You rehearse the Scriptures. You name the covenant.

Blessing is not something you chase. It is something that rests where order remains. You cannot demand what you have disordered. You cannot claim what you have fractured. You cannot host what you will not govern.

Scripture says, "Where the people are one, there the Lord commanded the blessing." *One* does not mean identical. *One* does not mean emotional agreement. *One* does not mean noise in the same direction. *One* means aligned, ordered. *One* means **whole** under rightful authority.

Where there is rivalry, envy, jealousy, and strife, blessing waits. Where there is hidden disorder, blessing withholds. Where there is fractured structure, blessing does not settle. Blessing is responsive to order.

You ask, "Why am I not blessed?" The deeper question is, Is there unity within you? Is your spirit aligned with Truth? Is your appetite governed? Is your authority intact? Is your house divided against itself?

The command is not given to chaos. The command is given to order. When Heaven finds structure, it releases supply. When Heaven finds alignment, it authorizes increase. Blessing does not land randomly; it is commanded where there is wholeness.

You do not chase blessing. You build order. And where order remains, blessing rests.

THE CENTURION AND THE MYSTERY OF BEING UNDER

There is a moment in the Gospel of Matthew when Jesus does something rare; He marvels. It is not a miracle that causes Him to marvel. It is not power, or spectacle, or devotion. It is understanding.

A Roman centurion approaches Him — a man outside the covenant nation, a Gentile, a military officer accustomed to command. He asks Jesus to heal his servant, but then says something unusual, “I am a man under authority, having soldiers under me. And I say to this one, ‘Go,’ and he goes; and to another, ‘Come,’ and he comes.”

Most readers move quickly past that statement, focusing instead on the miracle that follows. But the centurion is not describing military structure for the sake of illustration. He is revealing why he understands how authority works.

He begins not with those under him — but with what he is under. “I am a man under authority.” That is the sentence. He does not appeal to his rank. He does not appeal to his power. He does not say, “I am a man with authority.” He says, “I am under.”

“I am a man under authority, and I say to one, ‘Go,’ and he goes…”
(Matthew 8)

The centurion is not explaining command structure. His words carry weight. His authority does not originate in himself; it flows *through* him because of what he is properly under.

This is the mystery many resist. Authority, in Scripture, is not self-originating. It is transmitted through alignment. It flows through positioning. It rests where order is honored.

The centurion understands that authority does not function because of volume, personality, or proximity. It functions because of structure. He does not need Jesus to come physically to his house. He does not require demonstration. He recognizes that when someone is properly aligned under Divine order, their word carries weight beyond their location.

He is saying, in essence, "I understand how this works. I live inside it. Because I am properly positioned under authority, what I say carries authority. I do not generate it; I operate within it."

This is not abstract theology. It is invisible governance.

The centurion's insight exposes a common modern error: the pursuit of authority without submission. Many desire influence, impact, and spiritual power, yet resist alignment. They want the fruit of authority while dismissing the structure that sustains it.

Authority without alignment is unstable.

In Scripture, being "under" is not humiliation. It is protection. It is placement within ordered design. To be under proper authority is to be covered by it. It is to function within a system where power flows legitimately.

The centurion does not feel diminished by being under authority. He understands that it is precisely why those under him respond. His effectiveness is not independent. It is connected.

This is why Jesus marvels. He does not marvel at the centurion's rank. He marvels at his recognition of order. The centurion sees something many within Israel had missed: that authority is relationally transmitted. It moves through alignment, not assertion.

This is an intangible reality.

You cannot see alignment. You cannot measure submission. You cannot quantify positioning. Yet these invisible conditions determine whether words carry weight, whether actions produce effect, and whether authority holds or leaks.

When alignment fractures, authority weakens — even if titles remain. When positioning shifts improperly, influence erodes — even if charisma increases. These changes are not always immediate, but they are structural.

Know this: structure always reveals itself in time.

The centurion's understanding places him in harmony with Divine order. He recognizes in Jesus the same principle he lives under: authority that flows from being rightly positioned under the Father. Jesus repeatedly says that He speaks only what He hears from the Father, and He does only what He sees the Father doing. Even the Son does not operate independently.

This is not weakness. It is perfect alignment. The invisible order between Father and Son produces visible authority over sickness, nature, and death.

Here is the deeper theological truth: authority in Scripture is covenantal before it is functional. It belongs within relationship. It flows through obedience. It rests on alignment.

To be "under" is to be situated within covenant structure. And covenant structure is an intangible reality that produces tangible effect.

The centurion is not merely an example of faith; he is a witness to the architecture of invisible order. He demonstrates that being rightly aligned under authority determines what responds to you.

Without that alignment, command becomes noise. With it, even a word spoken at a distance carries force.

This principle extends beyond military ranks or miracles. It governs households, leadership, speech, and spiritual life. Where alignment is intact, authority functions.

Where alignment is resisted, authority strains.

The modern instinct toward independence misunderstands this entirely. It assumes that freedom is the absence of being under. Scripture presents freedom as the result of being rightly under.

The centurion understood that. And because he understood it, he recognized it in Christ. He did not marvel at power; He recognized order.

Authority is jurisdiction, alignment, governance. While Intangibles are weight, trust, honor, credibility, covering, Peace, spiritual sensitivity, clarity, and relational capital. While these are real, they are not visible; they are structural.

WHEN YOU SHOULD BE UNDER — AND WHEN YOU SHOULD BE OVER

Confusion about authority rarely begins with arrogance. It begins with misplacement. Some people remain under when they are meant to govern. Others attempt to govern when they have never properly aligned.

Both create instability.

Scripture does not present authority as a fixed posture. It presents it as ordered placement. There are seasons and spheres in which you are under, and there are spheres in which you are over. Maturity is knowing the difference.

Being under authority is not a permanent diminishment. It is positioning within structure.

Children are under parents. Students are under teachers. Believers are under Christ. Citizens are under governing authorities.

This is not oppression. It is design.

To be under proper authority means:

- You receive instruction.
- You operate within defined boundaries.
- You are covered within structure.
- You are not the final decision point.

That is not weakness. It is order.

Remaining under when you have been promoted and not rising to your rightful place creates distortion. At some point, the child becomes a parent; now the one that was under is *over*. The student becomes a teacher. To not do that when you should is not pleasing to God.

For when for the time ye ought to be teachers, ye have need that one teach you again which be the first principles of the oracles of God; and are become such as have need of milk, and not of strong meat. (Hebrews 5:12)

The steward becomes accountable. Authority in Scripture matures. Jesus Himself modeled this rhythm. As the Son, He remained perfectly under the Father. Yet within His earthly ministry, He operated with authority over sickness, storms, and *spirits*. Being under the Father did not negate His authority; it defined its source.

You are always under God. You may be under spiritual oversight. But within your assigned sphere, you are meant to govern.

Confusion results when someone attempts to exercise authority in a sphere where they are not aligned — or refuses to exercise authority in a sphere where they are responsible.

Consider the household. A parent is under God and, perhaps, under civil authority. But within the home, the parent is meant to be over — not tyrannically, but responsibly. Abdication here produces disorder. Overreach beyond this sphere produces control.

The same is true in spiritual life. A believer is under Christ's lordship. Yet within their own appetites, habits, speech, and decisions, they are meant to be over. If they refuse to govern their inner world, they invite external governance.

This is where many stumble.

They want to be over outcomes, but not over themselves. They resist being under instruction, yet desire authority over influence.

Authority in Scripture is always sphere-specific. You are not over everything. You are not under everything. You are under what governs you. You are over what has been entrusted to you.

Misplacement causes leakage.

When you attempt to rule what is not yours to govern, resistance follows. When you refuse to govern what is yours, decay follows. Both are forms of disorder.

This is why the centurion's statement matters so much. He understood exactly where he stood. He did not attempt to outrank Rome. He did not resent being under. He recognized his sphere and functioned within it.

Clarity of placement produces stability of authority.

There is also a deeper spiritual application. You should be under Truth, covenant alignment, rightful spiritual authority, and Divine order.

You should be over your appetites, your speech, your reactions, your stewardship, or your assigned responsibilities. If appetite is over you, you are disordered. If ego is over you, you are disordered. If external pressure is over you, you are disordered.

The question is not "Do I have authority?" The question is: "Am I properly positioned?" When you are rightly under what governs you, and rightly over what has been entrusted to you, authority stabilizes. Peace increases. Clarity sharpens. Blessings hold.

When placement is confused, even strong personalities strain.

This is not about dominance. It is about order. The invisible reality of placement determines the visible reality of authority. Most people's exhaustion comes not from lack of strength — but from operating in the wrong position.

PEACE: THE GOVERNING CONDITION

Peace in Scripture is not emotional calm. It is covenant order.

The Hebrew word *shalom* does not merely describe the absence of conflict. It describes wholeness, completeness, structural soundness. It is the condition in which nothing is missing and nothing is out of place. Peace is not fragile sentiment; it is alignment holding.

This is why the priestly blessing in Numbers culminates not in wealth, not in victory, but in Peace. "The Lord bless you and keep you… the Lord lift up His countenance upon you and give you peace." Peace is the sealing condition of covenant favor. It is the evidence that order remains intact.

In covenant structure, Peace is not decorative. It is diagnostic. When covenant alignment is intact, Peace stabilizes. When alignment fractures, Peace is the first to signal disturbance. Not because God withdraws affection impulsively, but because order has been violated.

Peace functions like structural integrity within a building. You do not see the integrity itself. You see what happens when it fails. Cracks form. Strain appears. Weight shifts unevenly. The visible symptoms reveal invisible compromise.

In the same way, Peace reveals invisible alignment.

Jesus speaks of Peace not as something generated internally but as something given covenantally. "My peace I leave with you." This is not motivational reassurance. It is the transfer of a governing condition. Christ's Peace flows from His perfect alignment under the Father. It is the tranquility of ordered obedience.

This is why Peace cannot coexist with persistent misalignment.

A person may suppress conviction. They may rationalize compromise. They may achieve tangible success. But when covenant alignment is disturbed, Peace erodes; not instantly, not theatrically, but steadily.

Many attempt to repair Peace through circumstance instead of structure. They change environments. They adjust relationships. They pursue distraction. They seek relief. Yet Peace does not return because the issue is not external friction but internal misplacement.

Peace is not restored by control. It is restored by alignment.

This is why Scripture connects righteousness and Peace repeatedly. Righteousness is not moral performance; it is right positioning under God's order. Where righteousness is established, Peace follows. Where righteousness is neglected, Peace weakens.

The modern impulse treats Peace as negotiable. It is traded for urgency, access, opportunity, and validation. People override internal disturbance in the name of ambition or fear. They silence the signal rather than examine the structure.

Peace is not optional. It is protective.

When peace remains, clarity sharpens. Decisions steady. Speech stabilizes. Authority holds. When Peace is forfeited, discernment blurs. Reactions intensify. Authority strains. Peace is covenantal protection around the soul.

This is why Scripture warns believers not to let Peace depart casually. The New Testament language implies stewardship — Peace must be guarded, maintained, allowed to rule. It is not passive. It governs.

To "let peace rule" means to allow it to arbitrate. To treat it as an authority within the inner life. When Peace withdraws, pause. When Peace resists, reconsider. When peace stabilizes, proceed.

In covenant theology, Peace flows from being rightly under Divine authority and rightly over one's inner world. When either collapses, Peace becomes unsettled. When both are intact,

Peace anchors the soul regardless of external turbulence.

Storms do not negate Peace; misalignment does.

Jesus sleeping in the storm is not emotional detachment; it is covenant stability. He remains under the Father's will and over fear. The external chaos does not govern Him because internal alignment holds.

Peace is therefore not circumstantial quiet. It is structural order within covenant relationship.

Because Peace is intangible, it is often dismissed. People override it. They call it sensitivity. They accuse it of weakness. They silence it for productivity.

But Peace is a governing superpower.

It tells you when something is off before evidence appears. It alerts you when alignment has shifted before consequences manifest. It preserves authority by preventing premature action.

Peace is not weakness. It is strength without agitation. When Peace remains, blessing holds. When peace fractures, tangible stability eventually reflects that fracture.

The question is whether covenant order remains intact. Peace is the evidence. Guard it accordingly.

WHY WE DO NOT TREAT INTANGIBLES AS REAL

The greatest danger surrounding the intangibles is not opposition but neglect. Human beings are trained from childhood to respect what can be seen, counted, accumulated, or measured. We instinctively respond to what is visible and urgent. We recognize money as real, time as real, property as real, and reputation as real because they occupy space in the natural world and produce immediate consequence when threatened. The intangible does not command the same reflex. Peace does not demand attention. Alignment does not announce itself. Discernment rarely interrupts loudly. Because these realities cannot be weighed or displayed, they are treated as secondary—felt perhaps, but not guarded as assets.

Yet Scripture treats them as governing conditions.

This tension exposes something fundamental about human perception. The natural mind does not automatically register invisible realities as structural forces. It registers them as moods, impressions, or preferences. Peace becomes emotional calm instead of covenant order. Discernment becomes intuition instead of perceptual authority. Alignment becomes personal comfort instead of rightful positioning under Divine structure. When governing realities are reduced to feelings, they are no longer protected as property.

This is how barter begins.

Most people do not consciously decide to forfeit Peace. They trade it. They override a disturbance because the tangible reward appears immediate. They silence discernment because opportunity feels pressing. They stretch a boundary because the benefit seems practical. They do not announce the trade to themselves. They soften it with language. "It's not that serious." "I'm probably overthinking." "I can manage this." The vocabulary reduces the gravity, but the exchange remains. Something invisible has been surrendered in favor of something visible.

Because intangibles are not dramatic when lost, their erosion feels harmless at first. There is no audible alarm when alignment fractures. No visible receipt when discernment is ignored. No public consequence when Peace withdraws. Instead, the shift is subtle. A quiet restlessness settles in. Clarity dulls. Reactions become sharper. Effort increases. Nothing collapses immediately, which reinforces the illusion that nothing significant has been affected. But structure has shifted, and structure always reveals itself in time.

Humans often attempt to correct visible instability without examining invisible roots. They change environments, alter schedules, pursue new strategies, or seek distraction. Yet the disturbance persists because the issue is not external friction but internal misalignment.

Tangible life eventually reflects intangible compromise. What is not treated as real will not be stewarded. What is not stewarded will be weakened.

The tragedy is not ignorance of these realities but casual familiarity with their erosion. Many have grown accustomed to diminished Peace and normalized internal noise. They have adjusted to compromised alignment and accepted chronic strain as ordinary. Because the loss was gradual, it feels abstract. If the same individuals misplaced money or lost property, urgency would follow immediately. But when Peace is unsettled, they proceed. When discernment warns, they override. When alignment strains, they press forward. The intangible has been treated as negotiable.

This book exists to interrupt that pattern. It asks a sobering question: what are you doing right now? Are you guarding Peace or trading it? Are you positioned correctly or compensating with effort? Are you under what governs you and over what has been entrusted to you, or have those placements quietly inverted? Most exhaustion is not caused by lack of strength but by structural misplacement. When alignment is ignored, unnatural effort replaces ordered stability.

The intangibles are not imaginary. They are structural realities that govern tangible outcomes. You may not see alignment, but you can fracture it. You may not weigh discernment, but you can dismiss it. You may not measure Peace, but you can lose it. And when these are neglected long enough, tangible life eventually bears the evidence.

Awareness is the first correction. Before you can protect an intangible, you must recognize it as real. Before you can steward Peace, you must treat it as property. Before you can guard alignment, you must acknowledge it as structure. This book does not introduce new powers; it restores seriousness to what has always been entrusted. What you fail to treat as real will eventually cost you something very real. And what you consistently allow will eventually govern you.

HOW INTANGIBLES ARE LOST

Intangibles are rarely destroyed in a moment. They are eroded. Loss does not usually begin with rebellion. It begins with small permissions. A slight override. A minor adjustment. A quiet rationalization. Because intangibles do not occupy physical space, their erosion does not look catastrophic at first. It looks manageable. It feels temporary. It sounds reasonable.

But erosion is structural.

The first way intangibles are lost is through misalignment that is tolerated rather than corrected. Peace becomes unsettled, but instead of pausing, a person proceeds. Discernment raises concern, but the concern is reframed as fear or overthinking. Alignment feels strained, but productivity is prioritized. The internal signal is muted in favor of visible momentum.

Momentum can disguise disorder for a long time.

The second way intangibles are lost is through gradual desensitization. The first compromise unsettles the conscience. The second feels easier. The third no longer registers. What once disturbed Peace becomes familiar. What once required conviction becomes negotiable. The soul adapts to diminished alignment. Not because the structure has stabilized, but because the sensitivity has lowered.

Desensitization is not Peace. It is reduced awareness.

A third pathway of loss is misplaced authority. When a person refuses to remain under what governs them, they disconnect from the source of ordered power. When they refuse to govern what has been entrusted to them, disorder fills the vacuum. Authority is always relational and sphere-specific. When placement is confused, intangibles begin to leak.

If appetite is allowed to govern, Peace weakens. If ego governs speech, discernment blurs. If urgency governs decisions, timing fractures. These shifts are subtle at first. But structure responds accordingly.

Another way intangibles are lost is through constant exposure to disorder. Environments matter. Conversation matters. Input matters. When a person repeatedly exposes themselves to cynicism, chaos, manipulation, or moral compromise, the inner world absorbs strain. Peace is not maintained in environments where alignment is repeatedly violated. Over time, clarity dulls and internal governance fatigues.

The soul is not immune to atmosphere.

Intangibles are also lost through impatience. Timing is an invisible multiplier, but impatience forces outcomes prematurely. When something is pressed before it is aligned, the structure strains. Peace is forfeited in the name of speed. Discernment is overridden for the sake of immediacy. The result may appear successful for a season, but it rarely stabilizes.

Premature fruit is fragile.

Perhaps the most common way intangibles are lost is through silent trade. No announcement is made. No formal decision is recorded. But a choice is made internally: Peace is surrendered to avoid discomfort; alignment is adjusted to preserve access; discernment is quieted to maintain relationship; boundaries are softened to keep opportunity. The exchange feels practical. It feels necessary. It feels small.

But what is traded invisibly will cost visibly.

Loss does not always manifest as crisis. Often it manifests as strain. Effort increases. Rest decreases. Reactions intensify. Authority feels heavier. Clarity requires more energy. Nothing dramatic has happened, yet everything feels harder. This is the quiet consequence of structural erosion.

The danger is that tangible success can temporarily conceal intangible loss. A person may gain influence, income, or recognition while simultaneously forfeiting Peace, clarity, or alignment. Because the visible is increasing, the invisible loss is dismissed. But tangible growth without intangible stability cannot sustain itself indefinitely.

Structure always reveals itself.

It is important to understand that intangibles are not stolen by accident. They are surrendered by neglect. They are misplaced through inattention. They are weakened through repeated override. The loss may not be malicious, but it is cumulative.

And yet, because these realities are covenantal, they can be restored. Alignment can be re-established. Peace can return. Discernment can sharpen. Authority can stabilize. But restoration requires recognition of how loss occurred. It requires honesty about the trades that were made and the placements that were inverted.

Intangibles are not fragile, but they are structured. They respond to order. They weaken under disorder. They hold where alignment holds.

Understanding how they are lost is not meant to induce fear. It is meant to cultivate awareness. If you can see the mechanisms of erosion, you can interrupt them. If you can recognize the moment of trade, you can decline it. If you can detect misplacement early, you can correct it before tangible life reflects the fracture.

Loss is rarely loud. It is incremental. What is incremental can be stopped.

THANKSGIVING — A PRIMARY INTANGIBLE

Before praise, before worship, before power, there is Thanksgiving. Scripture says:

> Enter into His gates with thanksgiving. (Psalm 100:4)

You don't enter with performance, you enter with gratitude. Thanksgiving is the doorway intangible. when it's gone, you know it. You feel it immediately. Entitlement replaces gratitude.

Demand replaces reverence. Expectation replaces acknowledgment.

Then the Peace shifts.

You can do someone a solid. You can open a door. You can sacrifice time. Silence follows. That silence is not neutral. It is a loss of thanksgiving--, and that's just person to person; that is not even upward toward God.

Thanksgiving is not manners; it is alignment. It acknowledges, I did not create this. I did not deserve this. I did not generate this alone. I am receiving. That confession preserves order.

When Thanksgiving leaves, humility leaves. When humility leaves, order begins to fracture. Blessing rests where order remains.

See how it connects?

When Thanksgiving leaves, disorder enters. Not immediately or dramatically, but structurally. Thanksgiving is not politeness. It is acknowledgment of source. When you say thank you, you are not merely expressing manners. You are confessing dependence.

The moment Thanksgiving disappears, entitlement takes its place. Entitlement does not shout at first. It simply assumes, access, provision, Mercy; it ***assumes*** God. Assumption erodes reverence.

A generation that does not practice Thanksgiving will not recognize Grace. It will normalize it. When Grace becomes normal, Mercy becomes expected. When Mercy becomes expected, humility evaporates. When humility evaporates, order fractures. And blessing rests where order remains. You can feel the absence of thanksgiving immediately. It feels heavier. Colder. Unsettled. Peace thins.

Praise—, The Intangible of Recognition. Praise is not hype. It is recognition of worth. Praise declares: This is good. This is honorable. This is worthy.

When praise disappears, everything becomes casual. God becomes casual. Leadership becomes casual. Sacrifice becomes casual. Covenant becomes casual. And when everything is casual, nothing is **sacred.**

That is intangible erosion.

The loss of Praise is the loss of Recognition. Praise is not noise. Praise is recognition of worth. To praise is to say: This is honorable. This is weighty. This deserves acknowledgment. When Praise fades, everything becomes casual. God becomes casual. Covenant becomes casual. Authority becomes casual. Sacrifice becomes casual. When everything is casual, nothing is sacred.

The generation that reduces everything to vibe and volume will struggle to retain reverence. You can reinvent the music. You can modernize the language. You can adjust the format. But if you remove recognition of holiness, you remove the stabilizer.

Praise preserves hierarchy. When praise weakens, hierarchy blurs. And where hierarchy blurs, blessing hesitates.

Worship — The Intangible of Surrender. Worship is not music. It is alignment of allegiance. Worship says: You are greater. I am under. I yield. When worship leaves, self rises. And self does not produce rest.

Jeremiah said: "Ask for the old paths… and ye shall find rest for your souls." Rest follows surrendered alignment.

A generation that does not practice thanksgiving. They will struggle with praise. A generation that struggles with praise will misunderstand worship. A generation that misunderstands worship will redefine God. When God is redefined, ancient landmarks are moved.

Thanksgiving, Praise and Worship are intangible stabilizers. Thanksgiving preserves humility. Praise preserves reverence. Worship preserves alignment. When those three erode, Peace erodes. No one will know where Peace went. All these are intangible, invisible forces. You cannot *see* gratitude. You cannot *see* reverence. You cannot *see* surrender; but when they leave, you feel the loss.

Loss of Worship is the loss of Surrender. Worship is not a set list. Worship is surrender of self-position. Worship says: You are greater. I am under. I yield. When worship is replaced with performance, self rises. Self is loud. Self is expressive. Self is creative. But self is not restful.

Surrender to God is aligning.

> Stand in the ways… ask for the old paths… walk therein, and ye shall find rest for your souls. (Jeremiah)

Rest follows surrendered alignment. The refusal came next: "But they said, We will not walk therein." That is the sound of a generation unwilling to submit to inherited structure. Not ignorant, but unwilling. Remove the ancient landmark--, you will not immediately collapse.

You will simply drift. Drift is subtle captivity. It does not feel like bondage. It feels like freedom at first. But when thanksgiving leaves, when praise becomes casual, when worship becomes performance, Peace withdraws quietly. The leakage will begin, the crack, the fracture and ultimately, the collapse as structure is lost.

You will pray for blessing. You will quote promises. You will declare increase. But blessing rests where order remains.

Order begins with gratitude.

NOTHING HAPPENED — I GOT AWAY WITH IT

The most dangerous moment in the loss of an intangible is not the trade itself. It is the silence that follows. The ancient whisper in Eden was not complicated. It was not violent. It was not theatrical. It was a sentence that has echoed through every generation since: "Surely you will not die."

The argument was not that God had not spoken. The argument was that consequence would not follow. The suggestion was that structure could be violated without visible effect. That alignment could be fractured without cost. That covenant order could be bent and life would continue as usual.

For a moment, it appeared true. Adam and Eve did not collapse physically the instant they ate. The ground did not swallow them. The sun did not darken. They remained standing. Breathing. Conscious.

Nothing happened. That is the lie, because something had already shifted. Peace fractured. Alignment broke. Covering changed. Authority inverted.

They did not fall dead. They became aware of nakedness. Shame entered. Hiding began. Blame followed. The visible world still stood, but the internal order had shifted. Covenant placement had been violated.

Death in Scripture is not merely biological cessation. It is separation from ordered life. It is dislocation from alignment. It is structural fracture. But because the body did not immediately fall, the natural mind could conclude that the warning had been exaggerated.

Surely you will not die. That sentence still governs human reasoning. When Peace is traded and no crisis erupts, the conclusion is, "Nothing happened." When discernment is ignored and opportunity still advances, the thought is, "I was overthinking." When alignment is strained and tangible gain increases, the assessment is, "It worked."

Structural shifts do not always manifest immediately. In Eden, authority over the earth was compromised long before thorns emerged from the ground. Shame entered before labor intensified. Hiding began before exile was enforced. The internal fracture preceded the external consequence.

The natural man evaluates reality by visible outcome. If there is no immediate loss, he assumes there was no cost. If there is no instant punishment, he assumes there was no violation. If tangible life continues, he assumes intangible order remains intact.

Covenant structure does not operate on human impatience. When an intangible is violated, something always happens — even if it is not yet visible. Peace does not vanish explosively; it thins. Discernment does not disappear dramatically. It dulls. Alignment does not shatter loudly; it shifts. Authority does not evaporate publicly; it weakens.

Because the weakening is gradual, the mind says, "I got away with it." That phrase is rarely spoken aloud. It is internal. It feels like relief. It feels like vindication. It feels like proof that the warning was excessive, like the hurricane warnings that came for days and days, but no storm ever came your way.

The absence of immediate collapse is not proof of safety; it is often Mercy.

In Genesis, exile was not immediate annihilation. It was delayed consequence. In many lives, tangible fruit continues for a season after intangible compromise. Momentum masks misalignment. Success conceals erosion. Productivity distracts from fracture. The illusion is strengthened by time.

Nothing happened yesterday. Nothing happened last week. Nothing happened this quarter. Therefore, nothing will happen. This reasoning mistakes delay for permission, and it is why too many think that God is not paying attention. But He is; He always is.

The most serious losses in Scripture did not begin with spectacle. They began with small misplacements that appeared survivable. Saul retained his throne after partial obedience. Samson retained his strength for a time after repeated compromise. Israel retained prosperity in seasons of slow drift. But structure was already strained.

The erosion was underway.

The danger of "nothing happened" is that it trains the soul to ignore signals. Peace unsettles, but life continues. Discernment warns, but doors remain open. Alignment strains, but opportunity expands. The natural man concludes that the intangible was not real after all.

Surely you will not die.

Something always dies first. Sensitivity dies. Clarity dies. Tenderness dies. Restraint weakens. Conviction dulls. And because these are intangible, their death is not mourned.

This is how erosion becomes normalized.

The enemy's oldest strategy is not immediate destruction. It is delayed consequence. It is the cultivation of confidence in small violations. It is the persuasion that structural order can be bent without eventual cost.

The tragedy is not that people are deceived once. It is that they learn to trust the deception. When the mind concludes that nothing happened, it becomes easier to trade again. And again. And again. But covenant structure is patient.

What is fractured internally will eventually manifest externally. What is misaligned will eventually strain. What is weakened will eventually show.

If you believe nothing happened, you will not correct misalignment. If you believe you got away with it, you will repeat the trade. If you treat delay as safety, you will ignore mercy. The absence of immediate consequence is not proof that the intangible was untouched. It is often the final invitation to realign before tangible loss appears. Nothing happened — is the most dangerous sentence a person can believe.

Because something always happens whether you see it or not.

One morning, somewhere and at some time in the future a person wakes up and things are different—really different. It seems sudden, but it was not sudden; it was working all the while that person thought that nothing was happening.

Now the serpent was more subtil than any beast
of the field which the Lord God had made
(Genesis 3:1A)

HOW TO PROTECT YOUR INTANGIBLES

Protection begins with recognition.

You cannot guard what you do not consider real. You cannot steward what you treat as symbolic. The first act of protection is to acknowledge that Peace, alignment, discernment, and internal governance are not moods; they are assets. They are entrusted conditions. They are covenant realities. Once that recognition settles, behavior changes naturally.

Protection is not defensive living. It is intentional positioning. The most consistent way to protect your intangibles is to refuse unconscious trade. Every day presents exchanges. Some are obvious. Others are subtle. An opportunity may require silence where truth should be spoken. Access may require compromise where boundaries should remain intact. Urgency may pressure action where timing requires restraint. The moment of protection is rarely dramatic. It is the quiet decision not to override an internal signal.

When Peace becomes unsettled, pause instead of pushing forward. When discernment raises discomfort, examine instead of dismissing. When alignment feels strained, correct placement before pursuing progress. Protection often looks like slowing down long enough to evaluate structure.

Another essential protection is remaining properly under what governs you. Alignment with divine order is not automatic; it is maintained. Regular exposure to truth sharpens perception. Honest self-examination prevents quiet drift. Submission to rightful authority stabilizes perspective. To step out from under covenant alignment is to expose your intangibles to erosion.

Staying rightly under what governs you preserves clarity and strength.

Protection also requires ruling what has been entrusted to you. If you do not govern your appetites, they will govern you. If you do not govern your speech, it will fracture Peace. If you do not govern your reactions, they will destabilize alignment. Internal governance is not suppression; it is ordered strength. It is the steady exercise of authority within your own sphere.

Environment matters. Constant exposure to disorder dulls sensitivity. Repeated engagement with cynicism, manipulation, or moral compromise normalizes strain. Protection may require distance. It may require limitation. It may require withdrawal. Not because you are fragile, but because Peace and discernment thrive in ordered atmosphere. You cannot continually inhale chaos and expect internal clarity to remain sharp.

Protection also involves honoring timing. Not every open door is properly aligned. Not every opportunity is covenant permission. The discipline of waiting preserves structure. Impatience fractures alignment more often than open rebellion. To wait until Peace stabilizes and discernment clears is not weakness; it is maturity.

One of the most overlooked forms of protection is confession and correction. When you recognize that an intangible has been traded, do not rationalize it. Restore alignment quickly. Realign your posture. Reestablish boundaries. Reaffirm covenant positioning. Intangibles respond to order. They strengthen where alignment is restored.

It is important to understand that protection does not guarantee the absence of difficulty. Peace can remain while storms rage. Alignment can hold while opposition rises. Discernment can sharpen in pressure. Protection does not eliminate external turbulence; it preserves internal order within it.The goal is not comfort. The goal is structural integrity.

When Peace rules, decisions steady. When alignment holds, authority stabilizes. When discernment sharpens, consequences are avoided before they form. When internal governance strengthens, external pressures lose dominance.

You protect intangibles not by fighting constantly, but by refusing improper access. You protect them by honoring placement, correcting drift, and declining trades that cost more than they appear.

The world may not see the protection. It may not applaud restraint. It may not reward alignment immediately. But over time, tangible life will reflect the stability of what was guarded.

Because what is protected internally becomes sustained externally. What is guarded quietly becomes strength that does not have to announce itself.

POWER: THE INTANGIBLE THAT CREATES TANGIBLES

Power is one of the most misunderstood realities in spiritual language. It is either inflated into spectacle or reduced to personality. But in Scripture, power is neither performance nor volume. It is capacity flowing through alignment.

Power is not noise. It is effect. It is the ability for something to move because you spoke. It is the ability for something to hold because you stood. It is the ability for something to shift because you were positioned.

Power is intangible before it is visible.

In Scripture, power does not originate in man. It is entrusted. Jesus repeatedly makes this clear. He does not operate independently. He speaks what He hears from the Father. He moves as He sees the Father moving. His authority and His power are inseparable from alignment.

This is the balance. Authority is the right to act within a sphere. Power is the capacity to produce effect within that sphere. Authority grants jurisdiction. Power produces manifestation. But both are governed by alignment.

Then he called his twelve disciples together, and gave them power and authority over all devils, and to cure diseases. (Luke 9:1)

The centurion understood authority. But Jesus embodied power. And both realities flowed through being rightly under.

Power in Scripture is relational before it is functional. It flows from covenant positioning. When alignment holds, power stabilizes. When alignment fractures, power leaks — even if charisma remains.

This is why power cannot be self-generated sustainably. A person may produce temporary effect through force, manipulation, or personality strength. But covenant power produces durable effect because it is not rooted in self.

How, then, is power obtained? It is not seized. It is received. It is cultivated through alignment, obedience, and faithfulness within one's assigned sphere. Scripture consistently shows that power increases with stewardship. What is handled faithfully grows. What is misused diminishes.

Power grows quietly when Peace is guarded. It grows when discernment is honored. It grows when restraint is practiced. It grows when timing is respected. It grows when internal governance strengthens. None of these are separate from power. They are the soil in which power matures. The natural mind looks for dramatic impartations. Scripture emphasizes ordered living.

Power is sustained the same way it is received: through continued alignment. When a person steps outside covenant structure, the capacity that once flowed begins to thin. Not because God is unstable, but because power does not operate independently of order.

This is where many fall.

They assume past effectiveness guarantees future authority. They rely on former victories while neglecting present alignment. They maintain public influence while private governance weakens. For a time, nothing appears different. Tangible effect may continue. But eventually the strain becomes visible.

Power without alignment corrodes.

The question is not "Do I feel powerful?" The question is "Am I positioned properly?" Because true power is quiet. It does not need constant proof. It does not demand spectacle. It does not defend itself anxiously.

It produces effect because structure is intact.

Power must always remain balanced under authority. If power exceeds submission, it becomes dangerous. If power is divorced from covenant order, it becomes destructive. If power is pursued without humility, it destabilizes the one who carries it.

But when power flows under authority, it stabilizes environments. It strengthens households. It clarifies decisions. It shifts atmospheres without strain.

Power is not dramatic. It is structural capacity under covenant alignment. It always begins invisibly.

God hath spoken once; twice have I heard this; that power belongeth unto God. (Psalm 62:11)

WHEN INTANGIBLES RESTORE TANGIBLE LIFE

Restoration does not begin with visible change. It begins with internal realignment. When intangibles are restored, tangible life follows.

This is one of the most hopeful realities in covenant order. What was eroded can be strengthened. What was misaligned can be repositioned. What was dulled can sharpen again.

When Peace returns, decisions stabilize. You do not feel pulled in opposing directions. You do not strain to compensate. Clarity settles, and action becomes measured rather than reactive.

When discernment sharpens, you see and assess situations quicker. You withdraw sooner. You avoid unnecessary entanglements. The tangible result may look like “good judgment,” but the root is restored perception.

When alignment is corrected, authority stabilizes. Words carry weight again. Leadership feels natural rather than forced. You do not need to press outcomes aggressively. Structure does the work.

When internal governance strengthens, external pressures lose dominance. You are not controlled by appetite, fear, or urgency. Tangible life begins to reflect internal steadiness.

Restoration is rarely theatrical. It does not announce itself with fireworks. It reveals itself in steadiness. In decreased strain. In reduced noise. In sustainable progress.

This is how you know intangibles have been restored: effort decreases while effectiveness increases. You are no longer forcing what alignment can carry.

Scripture repeatedly shows that when covenant alignment is restored, tangible blessing returns in time. Not always instantly. Not always identically. But structure produces fruit.

This is not prosperity doctrine. It is covenant logic.

If intangible misalignment can produce tangible instability, then restored alignment can produce tangible stability.

The restoration of intangibles does not eliminate difficulty. Storms may still come. Opposition may still arise. But the internal structure holds. And when structure holds, outcomes stabilize over time.

What was once eroding begins to strengthen. What was once fragile becomes steady. What was once noisy becomes clear.

The invisible governs the visible.

The purpose of this book has not been to create anxiety, but awareness. You are not powerless. You are entrusted. You are not empty. You are structured. The most powerful realities in your life may not be seen, but they are not abstract.

They are either governing you — or waiting for you to govern them. When you treat the intangibles as real, tangible life eventually reflects that seriousness.

And what is restored internally will, in time, be visible externally.

THE POWER TO GET WEALTH

Before Scripture ever speaks of wealth as increase, it speaks of covenant.

In Deuteronomy, Moses reminds Israel, "You shall remember the Lord your God, for it is He who gives you power to get wealth, that He may establish His covenant." The purpose of power is not accumulation. It is covenant confirmation.

The power to get wealth is not independent entrepreneurial brilliance. It is not luck. It is not mere opportunity. It is capacity entrusted under Divine order for the preservation of covenant structure.

The word "power" in this context refers to ability, capacity, strength. It is an intangible endowment that produces tangible increase. But the increase is secondary. The covenant is primary. Wealth in Scripture is never meant to replace alignment. It is meant to serve it.

When God grants the power to produce increase, it is to establish stability within covenant purpose. It is not for ego enlargement. It is not for self-exaltation. It is not for detachment from the One who granted it.

This is why Moses immediately warns Israel not to say in their hearts, "My power and the might of my hand have gotten me this wealth." The danger is not wealth. The danger is misattributed power.

Power without remembrance fractures alignment.

Wealth without covenant destabilizes the soul. The power to get wealth, therefore, is an intangible capacity operating within ordered structure. It includes Wisdom, discipline, foresight, diligence, favor, relational alignment, and discernment. These are invisible before they produce visible increase.

If alignment is lost, the same capacity can turn destructive. Wealth accumulated without covenant remembrance corrodes. It inflates independence. It dulls dependence. It distorts placement. Power to produce is safe only when it remains under authority.

This is consistent throughout Scripture. Abraham prospers under covenant alignment. Solomon prospers under Wisdom granted by God — and begins to fracture when alignment drifts. Israel prospers when positioned correctly and declines when covenant order collapses.

The power itself is not evil. It is entrusted, and like all intangibles, it must be governed.

THE POWERS ENTRUSTED TO MAN

Scripture presents man not as powerless, but as entrusted.

From the beginning, humanity is given dominion — not ownership independent of God, but delegated authority within defined boundaries. Dominion implies capacity. It implies responsibility. It implies effect.

Among the powers entrusted to man are capacities that are intangible yet decisive. Man has the power of speech. Words shape environments. They bind and release, bless and curse, build and fracture. Speech is not merely sound; it is formative force. Yet because words are invisible, once spoken, their power is often underestimated.

Man has the power of choice. Free will is an intangible capacity with tangible consequence. Decisions alter trajectories. Covenant alignment is either embraced or resisted through choice. This power cannot be seen, yet it governs outcomes profoundly.

Man has the power of agreement. Scripture repeatedly emphasizes the force of alignment. Agreement establishes direction. It invites influence. It creates covenant bonds. Whether agreement is righteous or corrupt, it generates consequence.

Man has the power of stewardship. He can cultivate or neglect. He can multiply or waste. Stewardship transforms entrusted resources into increase or decay. It is an internal disposition before it becomes visible fruit.

Man has the power of restraint. The ability to withhold reaction, to delay gratification, to govern appetite is not weakness but strength.

Entire lives are stabilized or destroyed based on this invisible capacity.

Man has the power of perception. Discernment allows him to see before consequences arrive. When sharpened, it protects. When dulled, it exposes.

Man has the power of alignment. He can position himself rightly under Divine order or attempt independence. This single intangible placement determines the flow of authority and the stability of power.

Man has the power to create through labor, imagination, and faithfulness. Innovation, craftsmanship, enterprise, and cultivation all flow from invisible capacity before they produce visible outcome.

These powers are not autonomous. They are covenant-bound. They function rightly when positioned under God's authority and within assigned spheres.

This is why balance is necessary.

Authority grants jurisdiction. Power grants capacity. Alignment governs both. If power is exercised outside covenant structure, it destabilizes. If authority is claimed without submission, it collapses. But when power remains under rightful authority, tangible life strengthens.

The tragedy is not that man lacks power. It is that he often mismanages it. Because these powers are intangible, they are exercised unconsciously. Words are spoken carelessly. Agreements are entered casually. Choices are made impulsively. Alignment is adjusted quietly.

Yet each exercise produces tangible result.

This is the dignity and the danger of being human. You are not powerless. You are entrusted. The question is not whether you have power. The question is whether it is governed. Power exists. Power is covenant-bound. Power must remain aligned. Restoration restores capacity.

LOADED DAILY WITH BENEFITS

There is another intangible that most people overlook, not because they are rebellious, but because they are distracted.

Scripture says that God "daily loads us with benefits." Not occasionally. Not when we perform well. Daily. The language is striking. It does not say He occasionally grants assistance. It says He loads — as though something is placed upon us, entrusted to us, supplied for us each day before we even recognize it.

These benefits are rarely dramatic.

They are not always financial increase. They are not always visible breakthrough. They are not always answered prayers in spectacular form.

They are subtler. They are the breath in your lungs when you awaken. They are the clarity you did not earn. They are the protection you never noticed. They are the restraint that kept you from disaster. They are the healing in your body when you didn't even know you needed it. They are souls and emotions restored. They are the Peace that steadied you in quiet moments. They are the unseen preservation of your mind, your body, your household.

Tender mercies.

Mercy itself is an intangible. It is the withholding of consequence. It is the extension of Grace. It is the delay of judgment. It is the preservation of life where fracture was deserved. And because Mercy is invisible in its mechanism, it is often unrecognized.

We notice crisis. We rarely notice preservation. We notice loss. We rarely notice what was quietly sustained. We notice when something collapses. We rarely notice how much did not.

Yet Scripture insists that Mercy renews every morning. That benefits are supplied daily. That favor surrounds like a shield. These are not poetic exaggerations. They are covenant realities operating beneath visible life. Like all intangibles, they can be neglected.

The loss of daily awareness does not mean Mercy has ceased; God is faithful, greatly faithful. It means perception has dulled.

Gratitude fades first. Then entitlement creeps in. Then presumption settles. What was once recognized as gift becomes assumed as guarantee. The soul shifts from Thanksgiving to expectation without reverence.

This is another form of "nothing happened." Because the day continues. Because provision still appears, protection remains unseen. The natural mind begins to believe that life sustains itself.

Covenant life does not sustain itself. It is sustained. Every day that you stand is not proof of independence. It is evidence of Mercy. Every moment of clarity is not proof of self-sufficiency. It is Grace. Every delay in consequence is not proof of innocence. It is kindness.

The intangible of daily benefit is lost not by dramatic rejection, but by quiet ingratitude. When Mercy is unacknowledged, it becomes background noise. When benefits are unrecognized, they are treated as entitlement. When grace is assumed, alignment drifts.

Awareness restores humility.

Humility restores alignment.

Alignment preserves power.

This softening is not weakness. It is stabilization.

Because the same God who entrusts authority also supplies Mercy. The same covenant that governs power also extends compassion. The intangibles are not only structural disciplines; they are daily provisions.

You are not merely managing authority and guarding power. You are being carried by Mercy more often than you realize.

When this awareness returns, something steadies. Gratitude sharpens perception.

Humility protects alignment. Remembrance guards against presumption.

The loss of Mercy awareness is subtle. It looks like hurry. It sounds like self-congratulation. It feels like independence. But the restoration of awareness changes the posture of the soul.

Instead of striving, there is steadiness. Instead of entitlement, there is reverence. Instead of assumption, there is gratitude.

Daily benefits are not always tangible in the way wealth is tangible. They are often invisible protections, quiet preservations, unseen alignments, restrained consequences.

They are mercies. And they are real. To live conscious of daily mercy is to live anchored. To forget it is to drift toward pride. And pride fractures alignment faster than weakness ever could.

You are loaded daily. Whether you notice or not. The wise man notices.

GIFTS, TALENTS, SKILLS, AND ABILITIES

Up to this point, we have spoken of intangibles that govern humanity broadly — Peace, alignment, discernment, authority, mercy. But there are also intangibles that are particular. They are not distributed identically. They are assigned.

Scripture makes this distinction clear. Dominion was given to mankind. But gifts are given individually.

A gift is not learned first. It is recognized. It may be developed, strengthened, refined, but its root is granted. Talent is similar — a natural inclination or capacity that seems to operate with less strain than other efforts. Skill, while developed through repetition and discipline, still depends upon an internal capacity to grow. Ability is the convergence of design and development.

All of these are intangible before they become visible.

You cannot see a gift until it is expressed. You cannot measure talent until it is applied. You cannot weigh skill until it produces something tangible. Yet the invisible capacity precedes the visible result.

Scripture treats gifts as entrusted stewardship, not personal possession. In the parables of Jesus, servants are given talents — not owned, but entrusted. They are expected to cultivate, multiply, and present increase. The issue is not who received more or less. The issue is whether what was given was developed.

Gifts do not disappear dramatically. They diminish through neglect.

A capacity that is never exercised dulls. A skill that is never sharpened weakens. A calling that is never embraced becomes quieter in perception, even if it remains present in design.

Loss here is rarely theft. It is disuse.

There is also another danger: misalignment of gift. When a person attempts to use what was given outside covenant positioning, strain increases. A gift may still function, but peace weakens. Effect may remain, but joy thins. Because gifts are meant to operate under alignment, not independent of it.

It is possible to possess talent and lack stability. It is possible to exercise skill and feel empty. It is possible to operate ability and still sense erosion. Because gifts are not the foundation. Alignment is.

But when gifts are stewarded properly — under authority, within alignment, with gratitude — they grow. They mature. They deepen. What once required effort begins to flow with steadiness.

Gifts are intangible capacities that create tangible impact. And like all intangibles, they must be guarded from neglect, pride, misuse, and comparison.

You were not made generically. You were entrusted specifically. What is entrusted must be stewarded.

The warning here is to guard against any trades with the dark kingdom. By now you should see how precious you are to God and all the blessings He has given you. You should not be willing to lose even one of your God-given Graces. So walk wisely.

ANOINTING — AND THE LOVE TO WORK WHAT YOU HAVE BEEN GIVEN

There is a difference between gift and anointing.

A gift is capacity; Anointing is empowerment. A gift may exist without maturity. Anointing rests where alignment and purpose converge.

In Scripture, anointing is not theatrical. It is the presence of divine enablement upon a person for a specific function. It cannot be manufactured. It cannot be faked sustainably. It rests, and when it rests, effectiveness increases beyond natural capacity.

Yet even anointing is not self-sustaining.

Samson is a sobering example. Strength operated through him repeatedly. Victory followed him. Power manifested visibly. But alignment deteriorated quietly. And when the moment came, the text says he did not know that the Lord had departed from him.

Anointing can lift. And it can lift off. Not because God is unstable. But because anointing rests within covenant alignment.

There is also another intangible rarely discussed: Love. Many of the gifts work by Love, pure, agape Love; you need it to work the gifts you have been given.

Many begin with zeal. They feel alive within their gift. They labor with joy. But over time, comparison, distraction, or fatigue dulls affection. The capacity remains, but the delight weakens.

When Love diminishes, stewardship weakens.

The joy of working your gift is itself an intangible Mercy. It fuels discipline. It sustains perseverance. It guards against burnout. When that joy is neglected or traded for ambition alone, the gift may continue functioning, but the soul begins to strain.

Anointing and affection for one's assignment must both be guarded. Alignment preserves anointing. Gratitude preserves joy. Humility preserves sustainability. When these are maintained, what you carry strengthens over time.

When neglected, the loss may not be immediate, but it will be felt.

THE FRUITS THAT CAN BE DIMINISHED

The fruits of the Spirit are often treated as permanent personality traits. But Scripture presents them as evidence of ongoing alignment.

Love, joy, Peace, patience, gentleness, goodness, faithfulness, meekness, self-control — these are not decorative virtues. They are manifestations of life flowing properly through the soul.

They are intangible. You cannot see patience until it is tested. You cannot see gentleness until it is required. You cannot see self-control until temptation presses.

Yet these virtues can thin. They may not vanish instantly, but they can weaken. Even if you fall into sin once, get up, repent and walk uprightly before the Lord. Repeated sin means repeated thinning of your gifts and virtues. The devil will not stop unless you stop him. You can stop him by resisting him. That means resisting temptation and resisting sin. If he has nothing in you, he will leave.

Jesus once perceived that virtue had gone out from Him. Power was drawn legitimately by faith. The incident reveals something profound: spiritual substance is real enough to be imparted. If it can be imparted, it can also be depleted.

Virtue must be replenished.

Fruit grows where connection remains. "Abide in Me," Jesus says, "and you will bear fruit." The fruit is not self-generated. It flows from abiding. When abiding weakens, fruit strains.

Love can cool. Joy can thin. Peace can fragment. Patience can shorten. Not because the Spirit has changed, but because alignment and communion require maintenance.

Virtues are not immune to neglect.

They are strengthened through abiding, protected through humility, and restored through repentance and return.

The good things God gives — gifts, anointing, virtue — are real. They are powerful. They are entrusted. And because they are invisible at their root, they must be consciously stewarded.

Loss is not always loud. Diminishment is often gradual. But restoration is possible.

RETURN: HOW WHAT WAS LOST IS RESTORED

Nothing God entrusts is restored through denial. It is restored through return. If Peace has thinned, don't panic, it can be returned if you returned. That applies to dulled discernment, shifted alignment, thinned virtue.

The answer is: return.

Scripture does not whisper this. It declares it. "Return to Me." The restoration of intangibles is not emotional recovery. It is structural realignment.

You do not chase the fruit. You restore the root.

1. Acknowledge What Was Lost

Restoration begins with honesty. Not vague regret. Not self-justification. Not blaming others. Not with spiritual language that avoids clarity. Name it. Peace was traded. Alignment was stretched. Discernment was ignored. Gift was neglected. Even if anointing was presumed upon, or Joy diminished through pride or distraction, it can be restored. As long as there is life, there is hope.

However, you cannot restore what you refuse to identify. Prophetic restoration begins with truth.

2. Return to Right Positioning

Every intangible in this book rests on placement.

Ask:

- Am I under what governs me?
- Am I resisting rightful authority?
- Have I stepped outside covenant alignment?
- Have I assumed independence?

Restoration is often less about effort and more about repositioning.

The prodigal did not recover by inventing a new life strategy. He returned to the house.

Alignment restores flow.

3. Remove What Is Draining You

You cannot replenish virtue while continually leaking it.

Ask:

- What conversation is draining peace?

- What environment is dulling discernment?
- What habit is weakening restraint?
- What ambition is thinning alignment?

Prophetic correction removes access. Ask not in anger, but in Wisdom

If something is thinning what God entrusted to you, it must be limited or eliminated.

4. Reestablish Communion

Fruits grow through abiding.

Anointing stabilizes through communion.

Discernment sharpens in quiet.

Peace strengthens in presence.

Restoration is not performance. It is reconnection.

Return to prayer not as duty but as alignment.

Return to Scripture not as information but as positioning.

Return to obedience not as fear but as covenant intelligence.

You cannot manufacture spiritual substance. You must reconnect to its source, and that Source is God.

5. Rebuild Through Small Faithful Acts

Restoration is rarely dramatic.

Peace returns through small obedience. Joy strengthens through gratitude. Discernment sharpens through attention. Gift deepens through consistent practice.

You do not leap back into fullness. You rebuild alignment. Daily. Quietly. Diligently.

6. Refuse the Lie of Permanent Loss

The enemy whispers two lies:

"Nothing happened." and later,
"It's too late." Both are false.

If you are aware enough to recognize loss, you are not abandoned. Conviction is evidence of Mercy. Awareness is evidence of Grace.

Desire for restoration is evidence that alignment is still possible.

What was dulled can sharpen. What was thinned can strengthen. What felt distant can return. But you must return first.

7. Guard What Is Restored

Once Peace returns, protect it.

Once joy strengthens, steward it.

Once clarity sharpens, honor it.

Restoration without protection leads to repetition.

You now know how intangibles are lost. Do not re-enter unconscious trade. Go and sin no more.

The Prophetic Line

Hear this clearly:

You are not powerless.
You are not empty.
You are not finished.

But you are responsible.

The intangibles entrusted to you are real. They are not symbolic virtues or abstract ideas. They are structural forces that shape tangible life. If they have weakened, return. If they have thinned, realign. If they have been neglected, rebuild.

What is restored internally will manifest externally in time. This is covenant law. Return restores flow. Alignment restores power. Abiding restores fruit. Guarding restores blessing.

What you thought was lost may yet become stronger than before — because this time, you understand its value.

WHEN TO OPEN YOUR SOUL — AND WHEN TO GUARD IT

Guarding your intangibles does not mean sealing your soul.

Protection is not isolation.

A life that never opens becomes brittle. A life that always opens becomes depleted. Maturity is knowing the difference.

Your soul is not meant for universal access. It is not a public hallway. It is not common property. Scripture consistently treats the inner life as sacred ground — something to be guarded with intention. "Above all else, guard your heart," Proverbs says, "for from it flow the issues of life." The heart is not merely emotional space. It is governing space.

But guarding does not mean hiding.

The same Scriptures that command guarding also command Love, fellowship, confession, and covenant relationship. The soul is meant to open — but wisely.

How do you know when to open? You open where there is alignment. You open where truth is honored. You open where covenant order is respected. You open where peace remains intact.

Opening your soul in the wrong environment thins peace. It blurs discernment. It creates exposure without covering. But opening your soul in the right environment strengthens joy, deepens clarity, and reinforces alignment.

Not every listener of what you have to say is a trusted steward of your words, emotions or confidence. Not every confidant is safe. Not every relationship is covenantal.

The soul should open where there is evidence of stability, humility, and reverence for truth.

You will know you have opened correctly when Peace remains. You will know you have opened prematurely when Peace thins and clarity dulls afterward.

Guarding is required when:

- There is manipulation disguised as curiosity.
- There is pressure to disclose prematurely.
- There is dishonor toward covenant order.
- There is instability in the one requesting access.
- There is inner hesitation that does not lift with prayer.

Opening is appropriate when:

- There is shared alignment.
- There is humility and safety.
- There is covenant accountability.
- There is mutual stewardship.
- There is strengthening rather than draining.

Jesus did not open Himself to everyone. Scripture says He did not entrust Himself to certain crowds because He knew what was in man. Yet He opened deeply to the Father and faithfully to a smaller circle. Guarding and openness coexisted in Him without contradiction.

The same must be true for you.

Oversharing weakens authority. Withholding everything weakens intimacy. Wisdom chooses placement.

Your soul is not merchandise. It is not currency for connection. It is not leverage for approval. It is entrusted space. Open it where covenant strengthens you. Guard it where misalignment would thin you.

This balance preserves power without hardening the heart. The goal is not to become sealed. The goal is to remain ordered. An ordered soul is not suspicious. It is selective. An ordered soul is not cold. It is governed. An ordered soul knows that access is sacred, and sacred things are to be reverenced; they are not casual.

Epilogue

THE QUIET LIFE OF THE ORDERED SOUL

Most of what governs your life will never trend. It will not be applauded. It will not be measured publicly. It will not be obvious to observers.

The world notices spectacle, while Heaven honors structure. Man looks on the outward, while God looks in the heart.

You now know that the most powerful forces entrusted to you are not loud. They are not dramatic. They are not always visible even to you. They are Peace guarded quietly. Alignment corrected quickly. Discernment honored early. Power kept under authority. Mercy recognized daily. Gifts stewarded faithfully. Virtue replenished through abiding.

This is not a spectacular life, but it is a stable one.

An ordered soul does not rush to prove itself. It does not scramble for validation. It does not panic at opposition. It does not collapse under pressure easily. It is not because storms do not come. It is because structure holds.

You may not always feel powerful. You may not always feel anointed. You may not always feel clear. But if alignment remains, if peace rules, if communion continues, what governs you remains intact.

And when what governs you is intact, tangible life eventually reflects it.

The quiet life of the ordered soul is not fragile. It is not passive. It is not detached. It is deeply aware of trade. It is aware of placement. Aware of the Mercy of God, and of power. .

It is aware of return.

The world may not recognize that awareness as strength. But it is. The one who guards the invisible guards the visible. The one who stewards the intangible preserves the tangible. The one who remains rightly under and rightly over lives within covenant stability.

Nothing here required spectacle.

Only seriousness. Only awareness. Only return when drift occurred.

You were never asked to control everything. You were entrusted to guard what governs everything. And if you do that — quietly, steadily, consistently — your life will carry a strength that does not have to announce itself.

It will simply hold.

Amen.

I seal this book, all words, decrees, declarations and prayers herein across every realm, age, era, dimension, and timeline, past present and future and to infinity. I seal them with the Blood of Jesus and the Holy Spirit of Promise.

Let every retaliation against this word, these prayers, these decrees and declarations spoken, prayed, or said by the speaker, or heard by the listener, or anyone praying these words backfire without Mercy, to infinity against the evil perpetrator, in the Name of Jesus. **Amen.**

Dear Reader

Thank you for acquiring and reading this book, I pray it has blessed you to better understand the intangibles that make our lives work. God bless you.

Shalom,

Dr. Marlene Miles

If you enjoyed this book, here are some new releases

Christ of God (*The*) 3-book series

Christ of God, (*The*) Box Set, includes all 3books

Other books on Authority:

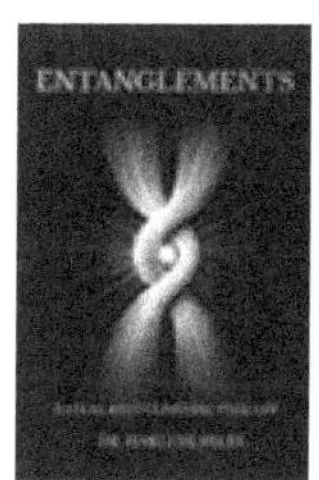

Prayerbooks by this author

There are some books that are only prayers. You just open up the book and pray.

Prayers Against Barrenness: *For Success in Business and Life*

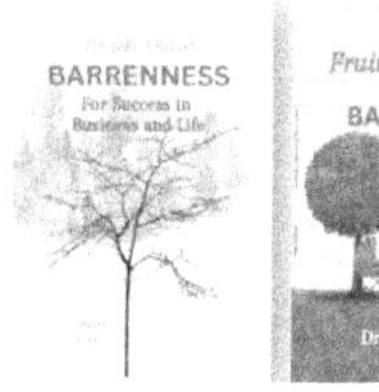

Fruit of the Womb: *Prayers Against Barrenness*

Beauty Curses, *Warfare Prayers Against*
https://a.co/d/5Xlc2OM

Courts of Marriage: Prayers for Marriage in the Courts of Heaven *(prayerbook)*
https://a.co/d/cNAdgAq

Courtroom Warfare @ Midnight *(prayerbook)*
https://a.co/d/5fc7Qdp

Demonic Cobwebs *(prayerbook)* https://a.co/d/fp9Oa2H

Every Evil Bird https://a.co/d/hF1kh1O

Gates of Thanksgiving

Spirits of Death, Hell & the Grave, Pass Over Me and My House

Throne of Grace: Courtroom Prayer

Warfare Prayer Against Poverty
https://a.co/d/bZ61lYu

Pray

er Manuals

FAKE FRIENDS: *Prayers Against Betrayers*

HOLIDAY WARFARE Prayer Manual (humorous) Surviving Family Gatherings All Year Long (without catching a case)

SOUL TIE Prayer Manual (The) Part of a 3-part series including a workbook.

MAD at DADDY Prayer Manual – part of a 3-part series including a workbook.

Healing the Sibling & Relative Wound Prayer Manual

Healing the Father-Son Wound Prayer Manual

Breaking Curses of the Mother Prayer Manual

Other books by this author

Abundance of Jesus (The)
https://a.co/d/5gHJVed

AK: The Adventures of the Agape Kid

Already Married in the Spirit: *Why You May Not Be Married in the Natural*

AMONG SOME THIEVES
https://a.co/d/dkYT4ZV

Ancestral Powers

Anti-Marriage, *The Spirit of*

Backstabbers https://a.co/d/gi8iBxf

Barrenness, *Prayers Against*
https://a.co/d/feUltIs

Battlefield of Marriage, *The*

Beware of the Dog: Prayers Against Dogs in the Dream.

Bless Your Food: *Let the Dining Table be Undefiled* https://a.co/d/6oPMRDv

Blindsided: *Has the Old Man Bewitched You?* https://a.co/d/5O2fLLR

Break Free from Collective Captivity

Broken Spirits & Dry Bones

By Means of a Whorish Father

Caged Life: Get Out Alive! https://a.co/d/bwPbksX

Casting Down Imaginations

Christ of God (*The*) 3-book series

Christ of God, (*The*) Box Set, includes all three books

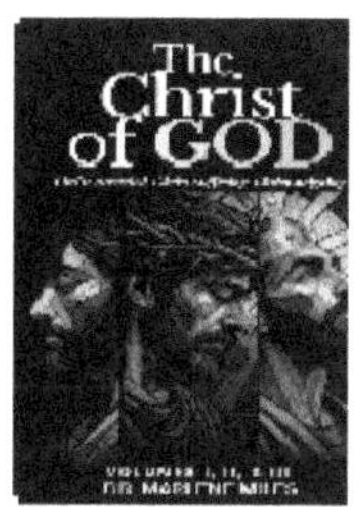

Churchzilla, The Wanna-Be, Supposed-to-be Bride of Christ https://a.co/d/eAf5j3x

Collateral Damage: *When What Happened Spiritually Was Your Fault*

Demonic Cobwebs (prayerbook)

Demonic Time Bombs

Demons Hate Questions

Devil Loves Trauma, *The*

Devil Weapons: Unforgiveness, Bitterness,…

The Devourers: Thieves of Darkness 2

Do Not Swear by the Moon

Don't Refuse Me, Lord (4 book series)

https://a.co/d/idP34LG

Dream Defilement

The Emptiers: *Thieves of Darkness, 1* https://a.co/d/5I4n5mc

Entanglements: Illegal Knots Limiting Your Life

Evil Touch

Failed Assignment

Fantasy Spirit Spouse https://a.co/d/hW7oYbX

FAT Demons (The): *Breaking Demonic Curses* https://a.co/d/4kP8wV1

The Fold (5-book series)

- The Fold (Book 1)
- Name Your Seed (Book 2)
- The Poor Attitudes of Money (3)
- Do Not Orphan Your Seed (4)
- For the Sake of the Gospel (5)
- My Sowing Journal

Gang Ups: Touch Not God's Anointed

Gathered: No Longer Scattered https://a.co/d/1i5DPIX

Getting Rid of Evil Spiritual Food

https://a.co/d/i2L3WYQ

got HEALING? Verses for Life

got LOVE? Verses for Life https://a.co/d/8seXHPd

got HOPE? Verses for Life

got money? https://a.co/d/g2av41N

Has My Soul Been Sold? https://a.co/d/dyB8hhA

Here Come the Horns: *Skilled to Destroy* https://a.co/d/cZiNnkP

Hidden Sins: Hidden Iniquity

https://a.co/d/4Mth0wa

How to Dental Assist

How to Dental Assist2: Be Productive, Not Wasteful

How To Stay Prayed Up

How to STOP Being a Blind Witch or Warlock

I Take It Back

In Multiplying I Will Multiply Thee

Into Freedom:

Irresistible: Jesus' Triumphal Entry
https://a.co/d/d09IfEC

KNOW YOUR BATTLE: Stop Swinging Blindly — and Win Against Opponents, Adversaries & Enemies (Workbook) https://a.co/d/eOwFKlV

Legacy

Let Me Have A Dollar's Worth https://a.co/d/h8F8XgE

Level the Playing Field

Living for the NOW of God https://a.co/d/6bK5duE

Lose My Location https://a.co/d/crD6mV9

Love Breaks Your Heart

Mad At Daddy: Healing Father-Wounds that Affect Motherhood (book, workbook & prayer manual)

Made Perfect In Love

Mammon https://a.co/d/29yhMG7

Man Safari, *The*

Marriage Ed.: *Rules of Engagement & Marriage*

Made Perfect in Love

Money Hunters: Beware of Those

Money on the Altar https://a.co/d/4EqJ2Nr

Mulberry Tree, *The* https://a.co/d/9nR9rRb

Motherboard (The)- *Soul Prosperity Series*

Name Your Seed

Occupy: *Until I Return*
https://a.co/d/bZ7ztUy

One Defining Day*: A Day When Dreams Come True*

Opponent, Adversary, or Enemy?: Fight The Right Battle with the Right Weapons

https://a.co/d/byQqEE2 & companion workbook: Know Your Battle

Plantation Souls

Players Gonna Play

Portals: Shut the Front Door: Prayers to Close Evil Portals.

Power Money: Nine Times the Tithe

https://a.co/d/gRt41gy

The Power to Get Wealth https://a.co/d/e4ub4Ov

Powers Above

The Robe, Part 1, The Lessons of Joseph

The Robe, Part II, The Lessons of Joseph

Seasons of Grief

Seasons of Siege: God Is Coming

Seasons of Waiting

Seasons of War

Second Marriage, Third--, *Any Marriage*

https://a.co/d/6m6GN4N

Seducing Spirits: Idolatry & Whoredoms

https://a.co/d/4Jq4WEs

Shut the Front Door: *Prayers to Close Portals*
https://a.co/d/cH4TWJj

Siege: *God Is Coming*

Sift You Like Wheat

The Silences of God:

Six Men Short: What Has Happened to all the Men?

SLAVE

Sleep Afflictions & Really Bad Dreams
https://a.co/d/f8sDmgv

Soul Prosperity soul prosperity series 3

https://a.co/d/5p8YvCN

Soul Ties: How Soul Ties Form, and How To Break Them (book, workbook & prayer manual)

Souls In Captivity

The Spirit of Anti-Marriage

The Spirit of Poverty
https://a.co/d/abV2o2e

Spiritual Thieves https://a.co/d/eqPPz33

StarStruck- Triangular Power series.

SUNBLOCK- Triangular Power series.

The Swallowers: *Thieves of Darkness*, 3

Take It Back

This Is NOT That: How to Keep Demons from Coming at You

Time Is of the Essence

Too Many Wives: *Why You Have Lady Problems*

Tormenting Spirits https://a.co/d/dAogEJf

Toxic Souls

Triangular Power *(series),* Powers Above, SUNBLOCK, Do Not Swear by the Moon, STARSTRUCK

TRIBE: *What Covenants Are Governing You…?*

Unbreak My Heart: *Don't Let Me Die*

Uncontested Doom

Ungovered Hunger: How Unchecked Appetite Dismantles Authority

Unguarded Hours, *The*

Unseen Life, *The* (forthcoming)

Upgrade: How to Get Out of Survival Mode
Toxic Souls (Book 2 of series) , Legacy (Book 3 of series)

The Wasters: *Thieves of Darkness,* Bk 2
https://a.co/d/bUvI9Jo

What Have You to Declare? What Do You Have With You from Where You've Been?

When I Was A Child, *I Prayed As a Child*

When the Devourer is Rebuked
https://a.co/d/1HVv8oq

When The Table Is Set Against You

WTH? Get Me Out of This Hell
https://a.co/d/a7WBGJh

The Wilderness Romance *(series)* This series is about conducting a Godly relationship and marriage with someone who is a Wilderness person. *The Social Wilderness*

- *The Sexual Wilderness*
- *The Spiritual Wilderness*

Other Series

The Fold (a series on Godly finances) https://a.co/d/4hz3unj

Soul Prosperity Series https://a.co/d/bz2M42q

Spirit Spouse books

https://a.co/d/9VehDSo

https://a.co/d/97sKOwm

Battlefield of Marriage, The

https://a.co/d/eUDzizO

Players Gonna Play

https://a.co/d/2hzGw3N

Sent Spirit Spouse (can someone send you a spirit spouse? This book is not yet released.)

Matters of the Heart, Made Perfect in Love https://a.co/d/70MQW3O , Love Breaks Your Heart https://a.co/d/4KvuQLZ, Unbreak My Heart https://a.co/d/84ceZ6M Broken Spirits & Dry Bones https://a.co/d/e6iedNP

Thieves of Darkness series

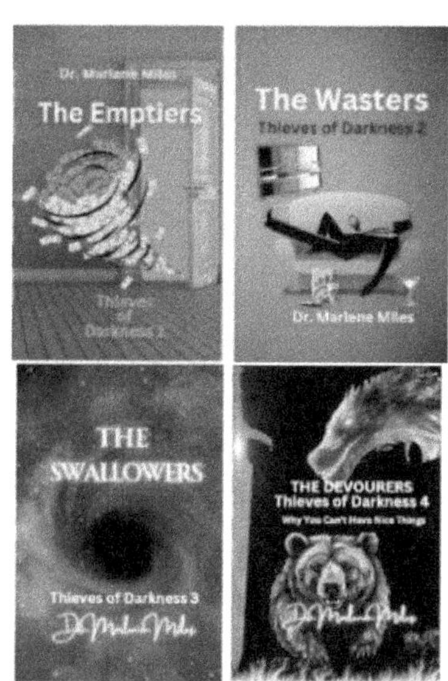

The Emptiers https://a.co/d/heio0dO

The Wasters https://a.co/d/5TG1iNQ

The Swallowers https://a.co/d/1jWhM6G

The Devourers: Why We Can't Have Nice Things https://a.co/d/87Tejbf

Spiritual Thieves

Red Flags: The Track Is Not Safe (book & workbook)

Triangular Powers https://a.co/d/aUCjAWC

Upgrade (series) ***How to Get Out of Survival Mode*** https://a.co/d/aTERhXO

We Get Along, Right? Compatibility for Couples – (book & workbook)

Dr. Marlene Miles is a teacher, author, and spiritual thinker known for her grounded, discerning approach to prayer and spiritual formation. Her work emphasizes clarity, restraint, and maturity in faith—helping believers move beyond emotionalism and performance into a steady, practiced walk with God.

With a deep respect for Scripture and a practical understanding of daily life, Dr. Miles writes for those who want their prayer life to be formed, not dramatized. Her teaching encourages spiritual maintenance, discernment, and responsibility—so faith remains strong not only in crisis, but in everyday living.